Contents

Lots of dogs

I **earn my living** by walking other people's dogs. Most of the dogs' owners work during the day so they can't take their dogs for a walk themselves. I walk several groups of dogs.

This is one of my regular groups of dogs.

Diary of a Dog Walker

Angela Royston

Raintree

Raintree is an imprint of Capstone Global Library Limited, a company incorporated in England and Wales having its registered office at 7 Pilgrim Street, London, EC4V 6LB – Registered company number: 6695582

www.raintreepublishers.co.uk
myorders@raintreepublishers.co.uk

Edited by Daniel Nunn, Rebecca Rissman, and Catherine Veitch
Designed by Cynthia Della-Rovere
Picture research by Ruth Blair
Production by Victoria Fitzgerald
Originated by Capstone Global Library Ltd
Printed and bound in China by South China Printing Company Ltd

ISBN 978 1 406 26065 6 (hardback)
17 16 15 14 13
10 9 8 7 6 5 4 3 2 1

ISBN 978 1 406 26072 4 (paperback)
18 17 16 15 14
10 9 8 7 6 5 4 3 2 1

British Library Cataloguing in Publication Data
Royston, Angela.
Diary of a dog walker.
636.7'083-dc23
A full catalogue record for this book is available from the British Library.

Acknowledgements
We would like to thank the following for permission to reproduce photographs: Corbis pp. 6 (© DK Limited), 8 (© Juice Images), 13 (© VStock LLC/Tetra Images), 22 (© Cristina Estadella), 23 (© Ocean), 24 (© Lawrence Manning); Getty Images pp. 4 (Flickr), 18 (Ingrid Firmhofer), 20 (Nick Ridley/Oxford Scientific); Shutterstock pp. title page (© Javier Brosch), contents page (© Lobke Peers), 5 (© Christian Mueller), 7 (© leungchopan), 10 (© Alexander Chaikin), 12 (© cynoclub), 14 (© piotrwzk), 15 (© tim elliott), 16 (© zhu difeng), 19 (© Dmitriy Shironosov), 21 (© Monkey Business Images), 25 (© Lobke Peers), 26 (© Elena Elisseeva), 27 (© Gina Callaway), 28 pen (© Piligrim), 28 diary (© Shchipkova Elena); Superstock pp. 9 (Pietro Scozzari / age fotostock), 11 (F1 ONLINE), 17 (Juniors).

Background and design features reproduced with permission of Shutterstock. Cover photograph of woman walking dogs reproduced with permission of Getty Images (Brand X Pictures).

We would like to thank Emily Brummer for her invaluable help in the preparation of this book.

Some words are shown in bold, **like this**. You can find out what they mean by looking in the Glossary.

The dogs never get tired of chasing the ball and bringing it back to me!

I take the dogs to one of the local parks.
The dogs run about and sniff all the smells.
I enjoy my work and have decided to
keep a diary to tell you about it.

Dashing dogs

Tuesday 12 June

As usual, I picked up each dog from its home. As soon as they saw me, the dogs knew they were going for a walk. They jumped into my car and off we went.

The cages at the back of my car stop the dogs jumping into the front.

When I let the dogs out, they were very excited. Cindy the dachshund ran off – but she came back at once when I blew the **dog whistle**. I rewarded her with a **titbit**.

Meeting friends

Wednesday 13 June

My friend Tina is a dog walker, too. We often walk our dogs together. I know all her dogs, and she knows mine. We help each other when there is a problem.

The dogs like to meet each other.

She told me that she has to go to the dentist next Thursday. She asked me if I could walk her dogs that morning. I agreed because she always helps me when I need it.

Sleepover

Sometimes one of the dogs stays with me for a few nights. The owners know that their dog will be well looked after and happy while they are away.

Duke is staying at my house tonight. Duke's owner brought his bed and his favourite blanket and toy along with him. Duke soon felt at home and went to sleep.

A difficult day

Thursday 14 June

Today was a bad day! This morning a woman in the park said I had too many dogs. I explained that I am a **registered** dog walker and that I am allowed to walk six dogs.

The woman's dog was barking a lot.

She wouldn't listen, and her dog kept growling at Duke. Then I noticed that her dog had a sore paw, so I cleaned it and bandaged it. The woman didn't even thank me!

13

Rain, rain, rain

Friday 15 June

It rained heavily all afternoon today. The dogs didn't mind – they love the puddles and the mud. I had some very wet dogs to dry when we got back from our walk!

I always take each dog back to its home. I have keys to each house in case the owners are out. As usual, I made sure each dog was settled and had plenty of water to drink before I left.

Weekend at last

Saturday 16 June

Many of the owners walk their own dogs at the weekend, so I don't have so many dogs. I replied to my emails and checked that everyone had paid me.

In the afternoon I dropped into a local **dog show**. I met lots of my friends and we talked about dogs! I bought some things for the dogs from the **stalls**.

Wonderful walks

Sunday 17 June

I never go to the parks on a Sunday – they are too busy! There are always lots of people in the park, but on Sundays there are three times as many.

I drove to my friend Maria's place in the countryside instead. There is a quiet walk near her house, down a lane and across the fields. The dogs love it.

At the vet's

Monday 18 June

I took Sasha the spaniel to her appointment at the **vet** this morning. She had her **annual booster injection** to stop her getting dog illnesses.

The vet said I was good with animals and should train to be a **veterinary nurse**. She said I could work for them while I train. I'm tempted, but I need to think about it.

What next?

Should I become a **veterinary nurse**? I like being my own boss, so perhaps Tina and I should start a **business** together. We could employ other dog walkers.

Maybe we could build **kennels** and look after more dogs when their owners are away. It would cost a lot of money to build the kennels, but we would get paid well by the owners for looking after their pets.

Playing in the park

Tuesday 19 June

I took the car into the garage for some repairs this morning. I walked some of the dogs to the park. Tina picked up the other dogs for me in her van.

I met Tina at the park. We let some of the
dogs off their **leads**. Sammy loves the park.
He picked up a stick and ran around the
park with it.

The real reward

It took a while to walk each dog back to its home. One of the dog owners paid me today. He said how grateful he and his wife are that I walk their dog.

Being paid is a good feeling, but seeing the dogs tired and happy after a walk is even better. That's the real reward!

Writing a diary

I keep a chart of the dogs and the days and times that I walk them. Writing a diary is different. Your diary can describe your life – what you saw, what you felt, and the events that happened.

You can write a secret diary that no one else is supposed to read, or you can write a story in the form of a diary. You could even write an imaginary diary for one of your pets!

Here are some tips for writing a diary:

- Start each entry with the day and the date. You don't have to include an entry for every day.

- The entries should be in **chronological** order, which means that they follow the order in which events happened.

- Use the past tense when you are writing about something that has already happened.

- Remember that a diary is the writer's story, so use "I" and "my".

Glossary

annual every year

booster injection jab to prevent disease that is given to top up a previous injection

business organization that sells goods or services to customers

chronological in order of time

dog show competition between different types of dog. The winner is the dog that the judges think is the best looking of that type of dog.

dog whistle whistle that dogs can hear but humans cannot

earn my living make enough money to live on

kennels place for keeping dogs, where each dog has its own cage

lead strap that is put around a dog's neck to keep the dog under stricter control

registered approved of by the local council or other official organization

stalls temporary shop counters, where things are sold

titbit small piece of something tasty to eat

vet doctor for animals

veterinary nurse assistant who is trained to look after sick or injured animals

Find out more

Books

Are You Ready for Me?, Claire Buchwald
(The Gryphon Press, 2009)

Dogs (Smithsonian), Seymour Simon (Collins, 2009)

How to Speak Dog!, Sarah Whitehead
(Scholastic Reference, 2008)

Websites

www.animalleague.org/kids/cool_pet_facts.html
The website of the North Shore Animal League gives lots of
cool facts about dogs.

**www.bxkids.org.uk/web/site/BlueCrossKids/bx_kids_
home.asp**
The kids' section of The Blue Cross includes stories about
animals the organization has rescued, as well as games to
play with your dog and much more.

**www.guidedogs.org.uk/adviceandservices/children-
and-young-peoples-services/about-guide-dogs-
information-for-young-people/**
A website with lots of information for children about guide
dogs for blind people.

Index